MY *Vagina* DOESN'T DO THE DISHES

SUZANNE ARDEN

BALBOA.PRESS

A DIVISION OF HAY HOUSE

Balboa Press books may be ordered through
booksellers or by contacting:

Balboa Press
A Division of Hay House
1663 Liberty Drive
Bloomington, IN 47403
www.balboapress.com
844-682-1282

Print information available on the last page.

ISBN: 978-1-9822-7897-7 (sc)
ISBN: 978-1-9822-7898-4 (e)

Balboa Press rev. date: 01/24/2022

"BOTH LIGHT AND SHADOW
ARE THE DANCE OF LOVE."

— RUMI

CONTENTS

ACKNOWLEDGEMENTS

To Murray - my "soul" supporter

For believing in me when I did not believe in myself, for the sacrifices you have made to allow me to create my dreams, and for your patience and unwavering love as I learn who I am and balance my own masculine and feminine. I love you.

To Corinne Ball

For the absolute support in getting this book finished. From the stunningly beautiful cover to your endless editing – you made my dream a reality. I can never thank you enough.

To Lani Huesken

My light, my inspiration, and my mentor. You inspire me everyday to look beyond what my eyes see, to look beyond what I perceive as real. You taught me what divine feminine looks like, acts like, and embodies. Your input on this book was perfect and inspiring. Thank you.

SUZANNE ARDEN

I grew up in rural Alberta in a very masculine dominant household. My dad was a very masculine man, and my mom was definitely not what you would call feminine. Mom was beautiful and kind, but she rarely wore makeup, jewelry, dresses or acted in a way that could be called "feminine".

She worked hard, 6 days a week, for much less than she was worth, and still took care of her kids, her home, and her husband. Mom was not overly affectionate and kept her emotions in check at all times. We definitely did not learn emotional mastery at home.

Dad taught us how to take care of ourselves, we were strong, we could fight, we could defend. I rarely, if ever, wore dresses unless I absolutely had to, I lived in jeans and t-shirts, I had no clue how to style my hair and never wore jewelry.

The first time I ever felt feminine or anything resembling beautiful was my first wedding. I had a two-year-old and was almost 23 years old and I felt sexy and sensual and beautiful for the first time. The feeling did not last past that day but the memory of how I felt popped up over the next several years.

I still really did not start embracing my own feminine until this book started coming to me. The idea for this book started 5 years ago and I have been working everyday to be deserving of it. This book chose me to write it. I thought it was too bold, too daring, too "much", for me to write. I quit on it many times. It kept coming back. In my heart, in my soul, I know I am worthy of being this Author.

My journey over the last 5 years has led me to love myself unconditionally, to quit doing what was expected of me, and to quit living an obligatory life. I went from working in an office for 15 years to writing this book, starting my own company, and choosing happiness.

Living from my core values has taught me how to live a life I love, and love the life I live, inspiring others to live from love, compassion, and freedom.

As Always
Love

Suzanne

CHAPTER ONE

THE FEMINISM RISING

What is the definition of a house slave?
What is the definition of a house wife?

House Slave

> ~A slave who worked, and often lived, in the house of the slave-owner, performing domestic labour. House slaves had many duties such as cooking, shopping, cleaning, being used as a sexual slave, serving meals, and caring for children.

House Wife

> ~A woman whose work is running or managing her family's home. Her duties include caring for children, cooking, shopping, cleaning, and serving meals.

There really isn't any difference except that now we get to choose who and if we marry. I am not a feminist. In fact, I believe that feminists did more harm than good in the battle for feminine equality. Feminists wanted equality – they wanted to be equal to men in every way. To me embracing my feminine is about BEING more feminine, embracing those qualities, not fighting to be more masculine. I want to be beautiful, sensual, intuitive, loving, nurturing, and healing. I want to dance and enjoy ceremonies and embrace my divine feminine essence. I want to wear makeup and jewelry and pretty dresses. I need community and women and relationships in my life. I do not want to work in construction, lift weights, and play football.

Traditional feminists have created a society of women who feel like they must do it all; work, clean, cook and take care of the kids. They must contribute financially and still be the house slaves. We wonder why women are burned out, tired, depressed, anxious, living in complete emotional separation and self-medicating with pills and alcohol. We are expected to do it all and still be sex goddesses when we get to the bedroom.

Why is it that women still feel like we need to do it all? To prove our worthiness? Our society has changed. Woman do not always get to stay home and take care of the children and the house, most of the time this is not financially feasible. Why are men not stepping in and doing half the household work? Why are women trying to do it all? Last time I checked my vagina was NOT doing the dishes! Or vacuuming, sweeping, laundry or scrubbing the damn toilets. Women are NOT house slaves. We are equals in relationships, in partnerships and in creating and maintaining homes.

Before you get defensive – I know! I know that this is not always the case, I know some men do more than their wives, some do equal, and some get a decent high five for trying. I also know that some couples have certain roles – the male takes care of the vehicles, yard, house maintenance and the female takes care of the housework. And this is perfectly fine if it balances and works for both PARTNERS! Marriage is a partnership, teamwork, and a duo – it is not a dictatorship, a monarchy, or a master/

slave relationship. Marriage is about mutual respect for what each person contributes to the home/family life. Marriage without respect is doomed, marriage where there is control and manipulation? Doomed. Marriage is about love, respect, family, laughter, and possibilities! It should be fun and adventurous and exciting (yes – even after 30+ years) and if it is not what is the point?

As we try to navigate our masculine and feminine roles in this new world, we have forgotten who we are. Men and women. Masculine and feminine. We have been taught that we have to struggle so hard just to survive, that we have lost our purpose, our passion, and our dreams. When one or both partners are so completely burnt out that they have forgotten what life is really supposed to be about and then the divorce talk starts, or affairs happen. Why? Why are so many people getting divorced now? Because women can no longer do it all. They are starting to break, to crumble, to fall apart and worse. They are starting to become numb. And numb is dangerous for everyone. Because we are fucking tired. We have been programmed to leave no time for ourselves to be feminine – we don't even know what that means anymore! We are missing a part of ourselves that we barely remember exists. We want to prove that we can do it all. We want to be the best wife in the world and take care of everything, including our husband and that is why we don't ask. That is why we cry alone in the shower. That is why we judge other women and ourselves so harshly. We are trying to be a woman that does NOT exist. We are not robots. We cannot work 40 hours a week, keep a spotless house, take care of our children, cook, shop, take care of ourselves and take care of our husband and still have friends. Hobbies. Passions.

So, what gets eliminated? Hobbies and passions. And then friends. Next is self-care – no time to do yoga, run, hike, go to the gym, no time to do your hair, makeup, iron your clothes. You start to forget that you have dreams, you start to forget that you feel better when you take care of yourself. You will not ask for help because you see other women handling it, other moms doing better than you. You should be able to handle it! And this is just one of the small ways women betray each other.

None of us can do it all. Not one – and hold it all together. So now you are burnt out, tired, overwhelmed and feeling "less than" and now resentful. And this is when your relationship gets pushed aside. Who wants sex when we haven't shaved our legs, we still smell like toilet cleaner, and we saw him checking out some fitness model on Facebook®? We fake a headache, or our period and lay there beside the man we love, resenting him. And he does not even know it yet. This cycle can go on for years. We start snapping, ignoring, bitching, nagging and in all honesty sometimes the men do not even know what has happened. Just that the woman he once loved is now a crazy bitch that he wants to avoid. How sad for the marriage. How sad for the couple. How sad for the world.

If we just ask for help. If we just admit that we cannot do it all. If we release the control. If we surrender. If we support one another. Men are not mind readers. If we do not ask for help, if we do not speak up, if we do not admit that we have limitations then men are just going to continue to expect us to do it all.

Forty-hour work weeks were designed

for men who could come home to having a meal prepared, a clean house, his children cared for and a wife that was happy to do it all. That is no longer our society. Men are working more than 40-hour weeks, women are working just as much, and everyone is burning out. We need marriages to become equal again. We need our families to work together. "My vagina does not do the dishes, my hands do. Can you use yours and do them?" It's that easy. Ask for help. Control is another issue I see in women in the running of the home.

— *"He doesn't do it the way I do."* — *"I don't like the way he..."*
— *"It's not good enough."* — *"It's not the right way."* Let it go! Honestly let that shit go!

Woman have been hiding their feminine for most of eternity... we live in fear and pray for acceptance. Little pats on the head and a *"good girl"* sure beat shame and blame. Who are we looking for acceptance from? Whose standards are we trying to live up to? Our parents? Friends? Teachers? Strangers? Spouses? What if we choose our own standards to live by? Who are we really? Strip down the labels, we are women with wants needs and desires that we shove down to make sure no one ever sees us as weak. We have been told we are the weaker sex, unworthy of love, money, rights, or freedoms. We have been submissive in our fears, in our belief that it is all true, in our belief that we have no other option but to follow the herd.

Men have also been hiding their feminine – it takes courage for a man to step out of the traditional masculine roles and embrace his feminine side. Men are teased for cooking, cleaning, helping with kids and even for actually loving their wife. They are taught to take care of their families financially, their safety, their security, and their homes. So, what happens when a man cannot do all of that on his own? Does he feel like less of man? Unworthy? He has been told his whole life that these are his responsibilities. Can we see how this is destroying our men? Our children? Our fathers?

Our world is in pieces, we need to heal ourselves to heal the world. We, the feminine, must rise in our hearts and our compassion. This is not the time to roar, it is not the time to fight, or push. Women are needed now. Right now. Our wisdom, our gifts, and talents and our love are needed. We can no longer sit back and watch our world crumble and burn around us. We have watched what fighting, competing, and pushing has done to our world, it does not work. We cannot continue living and leading in the old way. We must first remember who we are and then rise up as we are – The Feminine Rising.

Challenges

1) What are 3 positive ways that you already embrace your feminine?
2) What are 3 positive ways that you already embrace your masculine?
3) What negative things come to your mind when you imagine the feminine?

Devote time to yourself every day. Choose to embrace both the masculine and feminine sides of you, learn when to push and when to soften and flow.

If you are looking for help with any of the challenges, there is a list of resources at the back of the book to help you easily access it.

CHAPTER TWO

SISTERHOOD

CHAPTER TWO — SISTERHOOD

Women have been turning on each other since before the burning of the witches. We have been trained, brain washed and manipulated into turning on each other, backstabbing, gossiping, and stealing husbands and in this we have lost the bond of sisterhood. We are envious, jealous, and petty when it comes to watching other women grow, shine, or rise up. We shut them out, talk behind their backs and call them names. Witch, woo woo, crazy, phony, fake, liar, we judge their looks – too fat, too skinny, too tall, too short. Too old, too young, too fake, too plain, too feminine, too masculine. Why are we so cruel? Why has it become so socially acceptable to be this cruel? Why do we feel left out if we are not up to date on the recent gossip? Why do we not defend our sisters? Why are we okay with this behavior?

The feminine essence has been shamed, guilted, made fun of, belittled, and destroyed. It was not witches that burned, it was women. Women who loved, who danced, who healed, who sang and who chanted. Women who made potions, laughed too loud or had red hair. Sister turned against sister, daughter against mother and friend against friend and this cycle still continues. We are so eager to turn our backs on each other so that no one is looking at us. We know we are not perfect; we know that if we turn our back – even for a second – that we will soon find a dagger there. It is absurd. And it is the reason patriarchy has continued its rule. Women cannot and do not trust each other. It is the best example in history of divide and conquer. How will women ever rise if they continue like this? How will women ever be taken seriously if they are seen as petty and cruel? How will our daughters and granddaughters feel about this legacy?

Who is going to change this paradigm? It is up to you. It is up to me. Walk away from the gossip, stand up for your friend, encourage your sister, be better, be stronger and be kinder. Quit shaming and blaming and guilting each other. Stop the jealousy and envy. We can show love, compassion, pride, and true friendship. We are the change we have be waiting for. We have to be.

Starting with yourself. Can you love yourself enough to stop comparing yourself to others? Can you believe that you are exactly who you are supposed to be, doing what you are meant to be doing, looking the way you look? We are not all supposed to be the same. We are supposed to look, feel, enjoy, love, and grow differently. This is what makes the world exciting! We all have our place, our appearance, our passions and our dreams and they are meant to be unique. You are meant to be unique. What a boring world it would be if we were all the same – if we looked the same and did the same things and had the same dreams. You are fucking perfect. You are perfectly you. Can you see that in yourself? And if you get to be perfectly you, does that not mean that everyone else gets to be perfectly them? Even if you do not understand them, or believe in them, or even like them, they get to be them, and you get to be you. Without judgement, guilt, blame or shame.

Can you just imagine the world for a minute if we quit manipulating, controlling, and judging each other? Can you imagine encouraging and cheering on other women like you would your daughter? Can you imagine if we quit competing and started rallying together? How powerful would we be? As mothers, as sisters, as friends, and as women? What if we struggle together instead of against each other?

Could we stop the hatred? The wars? The terrorism? Sex trading our children? Rape? Abuse? Starvation? Slavery? Greed? The drug crisis? What could we do if we stepped together into our feminism? Into love, compassion, and loyalty?

Do not tame your wild, dim your light, quiet your laugh, dumb yourself down, shush your voice, dampen your beauty, hide your sensuality, creativity, sexuality, intuition, or power for anyone! Ever. Never ever be the reason that someone feels they have to dim themselves, hide themselves or behave! Be the change, the cheer leader, be the wild champion for the women in your life.

We have been so stuck in our self-sacrifice and self-sabotage as women that we believe in our hearts that we are small, ineffectual, weak, or unworthy. We work at jobs where we are grotesquely undervalued, and we stay in these jobs because we do not believe we deserve better. We believe in scarcity and lack, and these patterns keep us living in burnout and depletion. It is time to do things different, it is time to be different. It is time to support each other, show compassion, and be the love, the light, the beacon of hope for each other.

Challenges

1) Choose 3 women in your life to support unconditionally.
2) Take this week to stop gossiping, backstabbing, and sabotaging other women.
3) How can you step up and shine your light – become the beacon for others to look towards?

Learning who we are without our masks, learning to be our authentic selves allows others to show up as they are. Let's begin supporting each other's strange, their different and their uniqueness!! Isn't exciting to know that you can be unapologetically you?

CHAPTER THREE

WOMEN
THROUGH HISTORY

As women how are we not outraged? How are we not fighting for ourselves? For our sisters? For our daughters? Are we so brainwashed, so ashamed or so traumatized that we just do not know where to start standing up for ourselves? For the feminine. For loyalty, for passion, for basic human kindness? How much longer will we tolerate the old beliefs that we are weak, small, or worthless?

We have been burnt at the stake, hung, drowned, and stoned to death for the crime of being a woman. We have been sold, bartered, and traded by our fathers, raped, beaten, and murdered by our husbands. We have been house slaves and sex slaves. We have been raped by our fathers, uncles, friends, strangers and even by men that we trusted. We have been forced into sex and sexual acts by men in power. We are told we cannot get ahead without sucking dick or fucking a man. And we do it because it is acceptable — acceptable to whore ourselves to the highest bidder. To whore ourselves to get the role, to get the recording, to get the book deal, the model shoot. We have been complacent in keeping alive the oldest occupation in history – even though most of us have never walked the streets or stepped foot in whore house.

Do you know that female genital mutilation is still a thing? This abhorrent practice is still preformed all over the world! They cut and mutilate the external genitalia or other female organs for non-medical reasons between the ages of newborn to 15 years old. The main reasoning behind this is to reduce a woman's libido so that she will not enjoy sex, or to keep her in fear that if she has sex before marriage she will be found out. It is meant to control women – plain and simple. To keep them afraid, to keep them modest and "clean". Where are the protests? The riots? Why is no one stopping this? We all believe that we have no voice, that women have no say! We feel like we won't make a difference. I know one thing for sure, we will never know if we don't try.

We have been thrown away and murdered for the simple fact that we were born female – not worth loving, not worth feeding or clothing. Worthless. Just a girl. And we wonder why and how we end up spending most of our lives trying to prove to ourselves and others that we are worthy of loving, of getting the job, going to school, having love, money, and happiness. We are so programmed, so brainwashed, that we actually believe that we are not enough, that we are not worthy, that we are not lovable or worthy of love. We are. You are. We can have it all. We are enough just because we exist.

We keep allowing men to hold the power, in our governments, in our hospitals, in the music and film industry, in sports and religion. I mean jeez thanks for letting me vote... but really how about a real change? I am not talking about women doing the same jobs as men and acting, dressing, and ruling like men, I am talking about women doing the same jobs as men and being women. Being feminine as we are designed to be. Embracing what makes us unique.

Our children are being raped, drugged, kidnapped, coerced, blackmailed, and sold. And still, we do nothing. We do not fight, we do not rally, we do not stand up for our daughters, our sons. We let the elite, the rich, the powerful set the stage. We let them believe it is ok. We let ministers and coaches and teachers and bosses think that we are ok with this. We continue to let them get away with it. We might share some mild outrage on social media, but we quickly move on to the next headline. Why? Because we do not want to see it, to believe it – not in my back yard!! YES, it is in your back yard. It is in all of our backyards.

As long as the patriarch stands in absolute power this will be our story, our inheritance to our children and grandchildren. The world is out of control. The patriarch is getting bolder, riskier, and deadlier. They know without a doubt that if people come together, united, strong and in their equal feminine and masculine energies that the reign of terror will end. They see it coming so they throw around more fear, more manipulation – they fear us. They fear our growing communities, they fear our passion, they fear loss of control. And they should.

We will rise together as women, as sisters, as humans, as feminine united with masculine. They can call us witches, or sovereign, or priestess, or goddess, or divine feminine, healer or medicine woman – but whatever name we are called, we can and will make a difference if we join together. Embrace each other in laughter and tears. Build each other up instead of tearing down. Shine our own lights so brightly that we are beacons of hope. Beacons of hope for the generations to come, for the children, boys, and girls to live in a world of equality. We aren't joining together to fight, to rebel, or to judge, we are joining together for peace, for harmony and yes for love. Love, gratitude, joy, and acceptance is how we will begin to embrace the feminine, the sisterhood.

Freedom. That is what I dream of. Freedom to be me, freedom from judgement, envy, control, fear, and manipulation. Do you dream of that too?

Challenges

1) Can you completely honour all parts of being a woman? Your body? Your gifts? Your cycles?
2) Are you more afraid of being judged than of living an unfulfilled life?
3) What parts of yourself are you rejecting? Criticizing? Hating?

As we walk away from our past traumas with our heads held high, no longer in shame, no longer in blame, and no longer in fear – we will heal. We do not need to relive it, we do not need to punish ourselves or others, we need embrace the change. We need to be the change.

TOXIC/WOUNDED MASCULINE

CHAPTER FOUR — TOXIC/ WOUNDED MASCULINE

What happens when the masculine is wounded? They become the "Toxic Masculine" and the toxic masculine thrives on power, control, and Patriarchy. These are our leaders, and have been for thousands of years. These aggressive, violent, emotionless, tough, insensitive, self-sufficient, discriminatory, heterosexuals who believe that they are entitled to sex from others, who believe that they have power over women, "weaker men" or less "privileged" humans. Toxic masculinity thrives on judging anyone or anything that does not conform and often becomes harmful when not obeyed.

We are seeing this in most of the men in powerful positions all around the world right now. It is terrifying to me that these are the people that we have "chosen" to lead us, to teach us and to protect and serve us. We live in a world where it has become acceptable to dominate over others, to be aggressive and abusive in our power.

The biggest problem with this is that they believe (toxic masculinity can be found in men and women) that this behavior makes them powerful. It does not. It makes them inhuman, cruel, toxic, and repulsive, but not powerful. They are scared. Scared that someone will take away their power, that they will lose their power, so they try to control people. They have no control, no real control over anything or anyone. No one does. The only thing we have control over is ourselves, but they have been using fear, manipulation, brainwashing, and lies that have kept people subservient for centuries, but people are seeing through it now. We are seeing through the massive gaslighting and manipulation. We are seeing it in our homes, in the media, the news, advertising, and in our governments. We are paying attention now.

I am excited for us to all learn how to stand in our own power. Our third chakra – the Solar Plexus – is all about standing in our own personal power. When you are in your personal power you have strong self-esteem, you have a sense of purpose, you are motivated and responsible. When you are in true power you have no need to control others, to be aggressive or to be domineering.

People in their personal power do not steal, manipulate, bully, or demean. People in their personal power do not commit tax fraud, or loopholes, they do not "hide" their money. People in true power do not crash the stock market and cause people to lose money just because they can. Powerful people do not take and take money (taxes) from people who are struggling to survive – just because they can. People who are in their power do not lie and create chaos to keep people scared and separated. People with real power do not need to try to control outcomes by lying, cheating, stealing, and manipulating. Real power is not in brainwashing, gaslighting or fear mongering. Real power is not in shutting people up, shutting people down and taking away our freedom of speech and expression.

If you need to rape, drug, manipulate, brainwash, bully, gaslight, steal, lie, murder, enslave or abuse another human to feel powerful you have no idea what actual power is. You have no idea that you are the problem, you are the toxin that is poisoning the earth. You are not the master, the leader, the commander, or the chief. You are the poison, and you poison everything you touch, everything you claim to stand for and everything you love. You believe you are separate, better, stronger, smarter, and more powerful. You are none of these. Spreading hate, fear and separation does not make you powerful. It makes you weak. The problem is when toxic masculine feels weak or is threatened it attacks. They attack and they become dangerous, and they will stop at nothing to get that feeling of power back. They will beat people, rape, steal, murder, they will drop bombs and light the world on fire. And make no mistake – the world is on fire. Old structures, old ways, toxic masculinity – it is all on fire, it is burning all around us – I say let them burn it down! It is time for a new and better world – now it is time for equality. It is way past time for it.

Having a false sense of power is dangerous for everyone around. Look at our world leaders, coaches, teachers, preachers, directors, agents, and government officials. They have been taking what they want from us, money, and sex usually and causing trauma, deep trauma to us and to our children. We have started to say no more. We have started to say, "me too". We have started to take back our personal power, but we have to do more! How is human trafficking still happening in this century? How come more and more girls are being drugged and raped in bathrooms and dark alleys? How come the number of women being mentally, physically, and emotionally abused are on the rise? How come the media is allowed to blatantly lie but social media accounts are being shut down?

People who speak up are mysteriously dying, disappearing, and effectively being shut up. Who is shutting them up? They cannot shut us all up, not anymore! We are creating our own platforms, our own investigations, we are not sitting quietly in our denial anymore. We have started to pull our heads out of the sand, we are finding our voices, and we are healing the wounded masculine. We have created a world that has taken the humanity out of being human and it is time we put it back.

Challenges

1) What are 3 ways you can put humanity back into your life?
2) Where does the wounded masculine show up in you?
3) Do you stand in your own personal power? Or do you give it away?

The wounded masculine needs love, compassion, and support. They were not born this way, they were also manipulated and brainwashed into believing in false power and control.

TOXIC/WOUNDED FEMININE

CHAPTER FIVE — TOXIC/WOUNDED FEMININE

Women no longer connect with the feminine. It is seen as weak, woo woo, witchy, too soft, or too fragile. We want to be strong and independent; we want to be taken "seriously". We do not want to be sexual or sensual because we have been sexualized or demonized for that for centuries!

— "*Slut, whore, tramp, sleaze, trollop, prostitute, easy.*" — "*Her dress is too short, too tight, too low cut!*" — "*She deserved to get raped....look how she dressed/acted.*" And we don't just accept this, we play a role, a huge role! We are the role – women doing this to other women! And on the other side — "*She is so frigid, ugly, heavy, frumpy, desperate, playing games, cock tease*" — "*Maybe if she put out more, he would not have cheated*" — "*If she sucked his dick more, he would not have left.*" How cruel. How heartless. We take away a woman's confidence, her desire to be feminine and then we crucify her when she is not a Goddess on her knees, or a Warrior in the bed. You do not get it both ways. You cannot shame the feminine and expect it at the same time.

Backstabbing, two-faced, gossips. That is what women have become. We talk shit about our friends, our enemies, and strangers, no one is safe from our judgements and criticism. I knew a girl whose husband had cheated on her and one of her "friends" said, "She is so stupid, all of her friends are laughing at her." My husband cheated on me. How many of my friends were calling me stupid for not knowing? How many of them were laughing at me when I took him back? How disgusting. Women laughing at and mocking each other, it makes me fucking sick. Maybe if this girls' friends had have told her instead of laughing at her and telling everyone else what was going on she would have trusted in her "community" and left him. Maybe she knew her friendships were not real and felt like she had no one else, no other options, or maybe she just loved him enough, loved their family enough to try to make it work.

I have four close friends left. Four friends who did not run for the hills when I started my business, started talking about my book, and started fixing my marriage. I will forever be grateful for their unwavering love and support! Jealousy, envy, and even doubt and disdain at what I was doing showed up in very surprising places. My husband, my four friends and my children continue to support me but most of my friends and family could not even bother "liking" or "sharing" a Facebook® or Instagram post to help me grow my business. Toxic Feminine do not like to see other women shine. Toxic feminine do not root for other women and Toxic masculine does not want to hear what I am saying.

The prostitute wound – this wound is asking you to whom or to what will you give your power. It is connected to your root chakra; your safety, security and groundedness. What are you willing to do for money? For comfort? For safety and security? Are you willing to sacrifice your dreams to stay at a job because it is secure? Are you willing to stay in an abusive relationship for the comfort of your home? Are you willing to sacrifice your values to fit in with the crowd or be in certain relationships? Have you ever sold out? Manipulated others to get what you want? This wound is in most of the feminine because we have been treated like prostitutes for centuries.

When the toxic feminine has the prostitute wound nothing and no one is out of her reach. She will use every ounce of her feminine charms, her sexuality, her sensuality, creativity, and her imagination to get what she wants, when she wants it. She will do whatever it takes to get the job, the man, the house, the money, or anything else she can dream up. She does not care who gets hurt; if she steps on people or what she destroys in her path. She is selfish and self-centered and only worries about her own wellbeing, safety, and security. *Femme Fatal* at its finest.

The *Damsel in Distress* is on the other end of the spectrum of the toxic feminine. The feminine that cannot do anything for herself, who needs a man for everything. This is the girl that makes the feminine look soft, weak, spoiled and dim. This is the girl that always needs to be saved, always needs a knight in shining armour to swoop in and save the day. She bats her eyelashes and men fall all over themselves to do her bidding. She uses her sensuality in a totally different way, she comes across as the innocent, the virgin, the prize. The damsel in distress is quite aware of her beauty and uses it to her advantage and to any unsuspecting man's disadvantage. They are usually quite calculating under that sweet mask they wear, and they are quite aware of their effect on the unsuspecting masculine.

The feminine have played the games, followed the rules, stayed submissive and turned on each other. We played the game well. Strong independent women do not get to be soft. They don't get to dream big or believe in magic and love and happily ever after. They wear suits and cover their curves and deny themselves any feelings of sensuality. They do not get to imagine and create and nurture... Except we are changing the game and the Patriarch are so busy fist bumping they haven't even noticed. The feminine are learning to play by their own rules, making their own way in this masculine dominant world. We have been trained to be more masculine, stronger, smarter, to take action, to go after what we want — so what happens when we combine our feminine with that? Our creativity and imagination, our love and compassion? When we find our balance, we will all be unstoppable.

Challenges

1) Where do you see the wounded feminine in yourself? Do you see the Damsel in Distress or the Prostitute?
2) Have you ever been a woman "scorned"? Did you set out for revenge? Did you play games or use sex to get your way?
3) Have you ever lied or manipulated to keep a man? A job? A friendship?

The toxic/wounded feminine need to know that their feelings are safe, that they are safe. They need to be loved just for being themselves, for the very essence of them. They need love and compassion as they learn to love themselves.

CHAPTER SIX

BALANCE

CHAPTER SIX — BALANCE

Can we ever find a balance of masculine and feminine? What would that look like? I think it would bring about a whole new world. So, what is divine feminine? What does the feminine embody? Motherhood. To me divine feminine is motherhood, not being a mom, but more earth mother, Gia – nurturing and taking care of the earth and all of her inhabitants. Love, feeling love for all living things, with the knowing that we are all connected – the butterfly effect. Compassion for the sick, the injured, the hurt, the betrayed and the misinformed. Intuition, our gut feeling, our knowing that something has happened or is about to happen, our instincts to make the right decisions. The ability to heal ourselves and others and the knowledge that nothing needs to be healed as we are all whole and perfect. Creating, dreaming, imagining, and inspiring are all feminine qualities – they are the qualities that birth new ideas, new inventions, new creations, and new worlds.

Dancing, singing, music, art, writing, celebrating, sacred circles and building communities – all feminine. Cooking, baking, raising kids, gardening, and keeping a warm loving home – also feminine. Sexuality and sensuality. Divine beauty and radiance. Flexibility. But didn't I say in chapter one that my vagina does not do the dishes? Is this not going against everything I have already written? This is the divine feminine – not women, girls, wives, or mothers. It is important to understand the difference, divine masculine and divine feminine are in each of us – they are NOT strictly male or female. This Yin/Yang or dark/light balance exists in all things. We were created to embrace, accept, and love both of these energies within us – until the toxic masculine created the patriarchy, we now live in. So how we find a way to live in balance?

The divine masculine is action oriented – it is the fatherhood energy – teach, play, structure, and boundaries. The divine masculine thrives on doing things and taking action, where the feminine energy is more passive and contemplative. Adventure, risk taking, gambling are all traits of the masculine – the traits that get things done. So, while the feminine may be the part that imagines and dreams new creation it is the masculine energy that gets it done, that risks it all to follow the inspiration.

Logical and critical thinking are traits of the masculine that keep things like finances, economies, security, households, businesses, cities, and countries running. Taking action, self-discipline, and confidence are traits of the masculine that keep things moving forward, that produce momentum, and bring goals and desires into reality. Leadership is thought of as a masculine quality but if all leaders led from both masculine and feminine – combining logic and critical thinking with creativity and compassion – can you imagine how well your household, your company, your city, your country would run? Could run? Will run once we learn balance? This is why most women do not do well in leadership roles – they try to lead fully in their masculine and come off as bitches and power hungry and are rarely taken seriously and why men in leadership end up abusing their power and losing credibility and loyalty.

Not many of us can carry exactly 50/50 masculine and feminine and most situations do not require an exact split. This balance is more about knowing when, where and how to use the wide array of skills and traits we have access to while using our masculine and feminine together. There are times that each can be of great service and times where they can be of great failure. Use your own discernment to decide when to use which trait and how.

I will give you a brief example. You are a boss (male or female, it does not matter) and an employee comes into your office in tears because she is feeling overwhelmed and stressed beyond her capacity. In your masculine you might give her a moment – tell her to go back to work, everyone is feeling the same way, it is just the way it is right now, maybe she is not cut out for the job, maybe her personal life is interfering, tell her she is overreacting, ask if she is on her period. In your feminine you may feel such empathy that you cry also, you tell her it's okay and let her leave (leaving the rest of the staff to scramble), talk shit about the other staff not doing their jobs, and tell her she is justified in her breakdown (whether it is true or not). And lastly using both – listening compassionately, offering creative solutions, asking how you can help, letting her know her concerns have been heard and coming up with a plan or solution that works for everyone.

Can you imagine a job where you were treated this way? You are feeling heard, understood, and been made a partner in the plans and solutions going forward. You feel appreciated and empowered. There is no shame or blame in this scenario. Would you not be a fiercely loyal and productive employee knowing that you are respected and valued? What if your town, province, or country actually listened? What if the politicians we voted for actually paid attention to us? What if they would listen with compassion, hear – really hear – our concerns, what if they came up with creative solutions instead of just taxing us more and more. What if they could come up with and implement radically inspired ideas in health care, education, government, homelessness, the drug crisis, hunger, and war? What if they quit thinking that throwing money at problems will solve everything? What if we quit "fighting" against everything? What if they used their intuition, their hearts, and actually made real changes? Imagine the world if the divine masculine and the divine feminine found a balance, a harmony, mutual respect, and acceptance? That is the world I would be proud to raise my children and grandchildren in.

We can accomplish this, and it starts with us. It starts with us paying attention to our feelings, our emotions and taking radical self-responsibility for our lives. Looking at the things we do have control over and making changes. We can change how we show up for our relationships, our children, our friends, and our communities. We can support each other and drop judgements. We can quit numbing ourselves by drinking, doing drugs, hiding in our homes, endlessly playing video games, watching tv, and scrolling social media! We have gotten so lost in these outside stimulants that we have forgotten to actually live our lives, to laugh, and dance, and play! We forget that life is a fabulous adventure, and we hide ourselves away, watching the clock tick and the calendar change and we stay the same – stuck in our numbness. Judging people from behind our computer screens and our phones, pretending that we are living Facebook-perfect lives.

Challenges

1) Try it for a week, it's a fun experiment! If you have a more masculine energy, try leaning into the softness of the feminine, into ease and flow, empathy, and compassion. Imagine sending love and gratitude out to everyone you see or talk to in your day. Wear a dress, some jewelry, some makeup, or high heels; whatever makes you feel softer, creative, sensual. Dance, flow, feel your own body! Go outside and connect with mother nature, feel her, embody her!

2) If you have a more feminine energy, try making quick decisions, make plans with friends or family, make a choice that you would normally let someone else make. Speak your mind with confidence and stand in your own power. Plan an adventure! If you tend to be codependent, try out a week of independence, if you're a people pleaser, try a week of putting yourself first!!

(I would love to hear how you make out with this!)

Trying to have a perfect balance of the two energies will keep you stuck! There is no right or wrong way to play with this! Just make it fun!

CHAPTER SEVEN

MARRIAGE

CHAPTER SEVEN — MARRIAGE

What the fuck is happening in marriage these days? Gaslighting and narcissism have become household words. Physical, mental and emotion abuse are now a common part of the package. Cheating. Holy shit does everyone cheat? Even not cheating-type people are cheating. Marriage no longer holds the vows it was intended to. Marriage no longer means until death do us part or in sickness and in health. What has happened? What are we teaching our children? What does it even mean to love someone anymore? And why do so many couples not even bother with it anymore? Why are we numbing ourselves?

Remember way back before women had to work outside of the home? I don't but I have heard glorious stories about it. The husbands worked 40 hours a week and if they worked longer, they got paid overtime. They did not have to bring work home with them or answer phone calls and emails on weekends and evenings. They got to come home to a clean house, well cared for children and a home cooked meal that was actual food. The wives got to take care of the home, the children, the meals, and the social life. Communities looked out for each other, and neighbours were often best friends. Sundays were for family. Grandparents, aunts, uncles, and cousins all gathered in celebration of being a family. Love and marriage and children were celebrated.

There was still a complete split of masculine and feminine but there was not the pressure for them to choose back then. Now most women have to work and still do all of the housework, men are working 50 plus hours a week and often bring work home with them, cell phones and laptops have made this possible and with being paid a salary they are no longer compensated for overtime. There are so many financial and social pressures that people are beginning to crack. Now we have the new forms of fear that we are exposed to, with fake news and the ever-present internet and social media. Maybe ignorance really was bliss. We live in a constant state of awareness – everything and anything that happens – lies and half-truths flood our computers and our phones with minute-to-minute updates on the horrors of the world. It is meant to keep us scared, to keep us in fear, to make us believe that "they" are looking out for us, that "they" are taking care of us, that "they" are protecting us. The question now is who is protecting us from them?

This Patriarchal culture has convinced us that our worth, our value is based on what we own and what we "do" for a living. In order to maintain this image that we have created as "perfect", we must push, hustle, over commit, and exhaust ourselves. Marriages are failing because we take our overwhelm, our failures, and our fears out on the person closest to us. We know they love us, so it feels safe to lose control with them. The problem is, that if you are constantly taking things out on each other, you break each other. The person you love most in the world, and you have broken them, or they have broken you. That is what "perfect" is doing to marriage. We need to learn to fight together, with each other, not against each other.

All of this is causing us to live in constant fight, flight, or freeze. Our nervous systems are crashing, we have no self-control, no emotional intelligence, no sense of right or wrong in our own homes. We are lashing out at our spouses, our kids and sometimes even our pets. We can no longer figure out who is right or wrong, what is good or bad and sometimes we don't even remember what we are fighting about. Stress destroys. It destroys marriages, families, children, careers, health, and your body. When you live in a constant state of fear, of hatred, of shame, guilt, blame or anxiety – you are no longer you. Imagine for a minute what our society looks like with so many of us living like this? With economic crisis, fear of the next deadly virus, fear of our neighbors, fear of our governments, fear of our money being stolen, not enough food, not enough water, fear of being beaten, mugged, drugged. Fear of being raped. We are being wrapped up in our homes, in solitude, because we are so fucking afraid. We live in constant fear from the media, the government, the internet, and the medical system. They thrive on our fear. They make a living off of our fear. They feed our fear.

The sad thing, is that it is not just these things we fear. We have been so programmed that we have to be somebody else's version of perfect and we are terrified of not measuring up or worse, not fitting in. I think above all else we want to belong, no matter what, we want to belong in our families, jobs, and communities, and we will do whatever it takes to fit in. Commercials have played on fears since they first came out – that is their strategy. You have crow's feet, buy this cream, your neighbour is better than you, look at his car, you need to live in this neighbourhood if you want to raise your kids properly... and then we compare ourselves to the perfect Facebook® families with their big houses, new cars, family vacations, straight 'A' students and cushy jobs. We believe what we see, and we compare, we judge and envy. Then we blame, shame, and guilt our spouses for not providing a perfect family like "them".

Isn't it easy to find a sympathetic ear on the internet? I had a bad day, my husband/wife doesn't understand me... online affairs are skyrocketing. When I started my business online, I had men asking daily to have affairs, telling me they loved me. Some were persistent, some were disgusting and most I think were just lonely. This world is lonely. When we lived in community and celebration it was not up to the married couple to be all things to each other. Couples had separate friends, couple friends and family to play different roles and people felt a lot less lonely. We need more in our lives than just our spouses to feel fulfilled and with the lack of community and the ease of the internet it has become way too easy to stray.

Husbands and wives know each other's weak spots, their sensitive areas, and their 'fuck off' buttons. When a couple are living through a pandemic and isolation and have no idea how to figure out what are truths and what are lies in the world, they take it out on each other. They fight, they yell, they scream, they call each other names and manipulate each other. Then they ignore each other and try to find a way to stop feeling the stress, the fear and anxiety and they start drinking, or doing drugs, they numb themselves with social media, tv or video games and then they become lonely. Lonely while the person they "love" is sitting across the room – probably lonely and numbing themselves with Netflix too.

Marriage began as a way to ensure the

continuation of the species, a "system" to handle property rights, and for the protection of bloodlines. It was an alliance. It was economic. The INSTITUTION of marriage. "Till death do us part" – It seems a little simple. People change, feelings change, and the world changes. Most people get married now because we love someone so much, we cannot imagine our lives without them. Love, respect, loyalty, friendship, fun, and passion are what usually bring us to the altar now. So, what happens when one or more of these fades or disappears? Do we settle in a life that does not fulfill us? If we learn to embrace our masculine and feminine, can we save our marriages? If we learn to love ourselves and respect each other, can marriage survive? I hope so.

Challenges

1) Ask your spouse for help when you need it. Do not be bossy or cruel, they will be learning a new way too.
2) Pause. Breathe. If you have had a bad day at work, or you're tired, or the kids did something to make you mad – stop. Make sure that you are not bringing these issues into your marriage. Ask for comfort, understanding, and compassion. Please do not take your shame, guilt, anger, fear out on your spouse.
3) Love. Respect. Honour. Create. Play. Adventure. This is marriage. Is it yours?

Let go of trying to control everything. You cannot control your spouse, their feelings, or their emotions. Support their emotions. Our emotions are what separate us from animals, from machines. Honour your feelings and your spouse's. Learn emotional mastery.

CHAPTER EIGHT

CHILDREN

CHAPTER EIGHT — CHILDREN

Oh, what have we done? What have we done? These children, this new generation, they are fucking brilliant! You want to call them lazy, entitled, uninformed? They know how this world works; they are born knowing and understanding more than we ever will. Why? Because of the shift. The shift that has been taking place for years. They see it, they feel it and they live it. They do not feel the need to follow the path of the ancestors, the old worn-out programs, and stories. They use their emotions as they were meant to be used, as a guidance system, as a map that keeps them on their paths. We (I am in my late 40's) were not taught this. We were taught to be strong (men and women) do not show your weakness, do not cry, cowboy up, suck it up, big boys don't cry, anger is bad, fear is bad, sexual feelings are bad. Bad bad bad. We grew up being shamed for our emotions, being guilted for sexuality and sensuality, being ridiculed for our dreams and our desires. We were not taught how to feel or that it was safe to feel, we were taught to pretend.

Pretend you are happy, pretend you want to go to school, pretend you want children, pretend you want marriage, pretend you like mashed potatoes, math, and your sister's boyfriend. Pretend that you do not masturbate, fantasize about the same sex, wish you were the opposite sex, or that you had an orgasm. Pretend you did not get abused, beaten, neglected, abandoned, or raped. Pretend that you are someone else. Because you are not enough. You are not worthy. You are bad, unlovable, disappointing. Do what you are told. Be who you are told to be and do not ever, ever rock the fucking boat. Do not make a scene. Do not embarrass us. SHHH. Children are to be seen and not heard. Do not under any circumstances stand up against and adult – you must respect them, they deserve respect. RESPECT your elders. Always. The teachers? The coaches? The preachers? Our uncles? Our bosses? These are the people we HAD to respect. The ones who were raping boys and girls, children, being raped by adults, by authority figures because we must RESPECT them. Because we were told to.

Respect is earned not a God-given right when you hit a certain age, or a certain profession. No one deserves respect – you can only earn it. Kids see that now. It does not give them the right to be disrespectful, but it does give them the right to use their own discernment of whether or not someone deserves it.

Our kids question everything! They do not just believe what they hear, they do not buy into the "because I said so" or the "because that is how it has always been done." They want real answers, and they ask big questions! They are not sitting back and waiting for adults to tell them what to do, they are figuring things out on their own. They want a better world; a better earth and they deserve it!

We should be teaching our kids to be brave, to be their own inner authority instead of teaching them to listen to others. We should be figuring out their dreams, their passions, their core values, and helping to guide them to live lives that they love instead of stuffing them into boxes and expecting them to live great lives. Instead, we put our expectations, and societies expectations on them and wonder why over half of children need to be medicated for ADD, ADHD, depression, and anxiety! The system is failing our children and worse than that? We are failing our children! Read that again – We are failing our children. We say that we would die for our children. How about living for them? How about taking care of the mind, body, and souls of our kids. How about taking care of ourselves? Being brave? Loving our lives? Loving ourselves? How different would our kids grow up if we were better? Stronger? If we treated ourselves the way we want our children to be treated? If we treated our spouses the way we would want our children to be treated?

We drug our children so that they will sit down and shut up. We take away their natural ability to FEEL! Our feelings are what make us human, and we medicate our kids so that they loose that ability? How about if we taught our kids about Emotional Intelligence? What if we learnt about our feelings and quit making kids feel weak, small, stupid, different, or bad? Stopping kids from being kids is cruel and selfish. Yes, some kids have "diagnosis" where they "need" medication to survive our structured systems, but should we try other things first? Diet? Exercise? Talking? Teaching?

What if we took radical self-responsibility and taught our kids to do the same? What if we quit blaming other people, situations and the world for our problems and owned our own shit? What are we teaching our kids about body image? About bullying? About following the herd? How are we teaching our kids to live in this world and not just survive it?

We could start by teaching them what feelings are. How to use them. That no feelings are bad. Why don't we start asking them how they are feeling and what their hearts want? Ask them if we are supporting them in a way that is helpful. Ask what they want. Ask ask ask. The world is different now. We do not always understand what they are going through and if we are piling on our shit, our dysfunction... it is no wonder they need to be medicated to survive. No wonder they are struggling. We are so busy numbing ourselves, denying our own feelings, shaming, and blaming others, living in fear of truly being seen, living in fear of what others think that we are not really living. So how can our kids figure it out if we are not guiding them? If their best teacher is some stranger on Tik Tok? Where are they getting their information from? Pay attention. Do they understand masculine and feminine? Do they see mom or dad pulling all of the weight? Do they see abuse? Do they see stress and overwhelm? What are they seeing and what is happening to their nervous systems when they see it?

Our kids are in a constant state of over stimulation. They have been desensitized to death and destruction through tv and video games, they are raised with an iPhone, iPad, video games and Netflix on demand, providing them with non-stop numbing and escape from reality. Our food no longer has the nutrients they need, they no longer have to use their imaginations, or their creativity to be entertained and physical education has become enjoyable only for the masculine energies of competition, strength, and fortitude. Do you know what happens when our kids' nervous systems don't function properly? They live in fight, flight, or freeze. They live in constant uneasiness, stress, anxiety, and overwhelm. We need to be step up as parents and learn how to help them.

Challenges

1) 1) Learn about emotions so that you can help teach your children – or other children in your life.
2) 2) Look at what you are teaching your kids about love, marriage, body image, relationships, and the world.
3) 3) Be willing to see how much they can teach you. I have learned so much from my kids! I learned how to show up in my life, I learned how to be brave – they taught me to shine my light.

Our children are our future – it is so cliché but so true. We can raise our children to dream, to create, to love, and to lead, to commit, and to stand in their personal power.

CHAPTER NINE

CORE WOUNDS

CHAPTER NINE — CORE WOUNDS

What are human's core wounds? These are deep, fundamental wounds and beliefs that we are taught since birth. There are many of them actually and worth looking into, but for the purpose of this book we are going to talk about four of them. The first one is *abandonment*, whether a parent or loved one accidentally left you at a grocery store, was late picking you up from school or completely walked out of your life, a friend or boyfriend left you or you were left out of things, or someone close to you died, you can have the abandonment wound. It is a fear of loneliness, of not being connected, of not feeling your enoughness. This wound will show up in your life by making you feel constantly left behind, believing everyone leaves, and feeling deep betrayal from others. You may be clingy, over giving, insecure and easily triggered by loss.

The *neglect* wound can be physical or mental. It can be that you were not raised in a home with food, stability, love, or other necessities. It can also be caused by emotional neglect, being ignored, being dismissed, or being treated as a pest, nuisance, or annoyance. This wound shows up as feeling stranded, alone (even in a group of people), lonely and unimportant. A wallflower that no one notices. You may feel empty, have difficulty trusting, lack self-compassion and self-love.

The *betrayal* wound is when someone close to you betrays yours trust and it can leave deep trauma. This can be anything from a parent leaving or being emotionally unavailable to a spouse cheating on you. Anything that breaks a promise, a vow, a responsibility, or a confidence can be seen as a deep betrayal. This wound shows up as attachment issues, suicidal tendencies, or physical pain. You may have panic attacks, nightmares, or substance abuse.

The *rejection* wound is usually from parents rejecting their children but can also be from other family members, teachers, coaches, friends, or spouses. It is the — *"You are not good enough,"* — *"You are not worthy,"* — *"You are not lovable,"* wound. If you do not know who you are, if you hide yourself behind masks, run away or tend to disappear into a fantasy in your head you probably have the betrayal wound. You may self-sabotage on a regular basis, have a hard time letting people get close to you, people please, or neglect yourself.

We all have some or all of these wounds, the abuse wound, and the prostitute wound will be discussed in other chapters, and we may have them too. We have been taught to be ashamed of these wounds and we do not talk about shame. Shame is something we think is unique to us, dirty, or unspeakable. We hide our shame in dark places and pray that know one ever sees it. It is time to talk about it. It is time to quit punishing ourselves for our feelings.

When the feminine is unable to love, nurture, and protect her children, core wounds become much more extreme. We are all so busy trying to be everything to everyone else that we often forget to take care of ourselves, our children, our families, or our spouses. We live in a high state of emotions most of the time and we have not learned how to calm our nervous system down. We shut down, we yell, we snap, we withdraw, we numb, and we quit. We are living in constant Fight, Flight or Freeze, and we are not taught how to calm the stress.

The feminine have lived in Freeze for centuries. Maybe for all of time. Frozen in a time where they were not worth anything. Frozen in a time where they had to do and be who they were told. We are stuck in this place of believing that the feminine is woo woo, witchy, slutty, crazy, unworthy, unlovable, foolish, silly, or intimidating. We have also been in Fight, from the very first woman — Lilith, not Eve — who was created equal to Adam, we have had to fight for our rights to be equal. Our right to be who we are. We have had to fight for our rights to even exist and God forbid use our minds. We fight against our own sisters – we quit protecting each other and we fight harder against the rising feminine than men do. Why are we so damn afraid of being seen as feminine? Is it because we are taught it is weak? Soft? We will do anything, including destroy each other to keep from being seen as weak. The weaker sex. We look at the psychics, the healers, the creators, the speakers, the intuitives, the Goddesses, the Divine feminine and believe that those gifts, those talents are just for the chosen, just for the a few. Definitely not for me or you... Who do you think you are? Phony. Fake. We do not believe that our intuition and creativity are for all of us.

Flight? Yes – we have run away from our truth. The truth that we are equal but not the same. That what makes us unique is what makes us strong. The truth of who we are. We are in a flat out run to make sure that no one sees "us".

The masculine. How the masculine has survived the cruelness of our world is sometimes beyond me. Fight fight fight! They have killed and maimed, hunted, provided homes, food and have been completely and cruelly diminished if they show one ounce of feminine. Love, compassion, ceremony, intuition, beauty, creativity do not belong in the Patriarchy. The masculine has been so oppressed and persecuted for showing any feminine traits that it is now just commonplace to browbeat each other.

Challenges

1) What core wounds do you have? Do you feel shame around them?
2) Can you forgive the betrayer, the neglecter, the rejecter and the one who left?
3) Do you live in Fight, Flight, or Freeze? Do you know how to reset your nervous system?

We are meant to live with love and compassion. When we forgive another person and take radical self-responsibility we find peace.

CHAPTER TEN

WE ARE NOT BROKEN

CHAPTER TEN — WE ARE NOT BROKEN

Femininity is not broken, it is not lost, it is not shameful or weak. Femininity is in all of us, male and female, we have just been programmed so deeply, that we believe that dreams and passions, and magic are childish and "embarrassing". That being in our feminine is fragile or delicate or soft. The masculine and feminine are meant to be wound together in each of us, in society and on the earth. We are meant to embrace all of the parts of us, not hide them away, stuff them down and feel ashamed or fear them. We have to break this spell, this old paradigm that tells us that intuition, passion, creativity, sensuality, sexuality, healing, nurturing, compassion, and unconditional love is weak, that it is humiliating and that it is immoral, or degrading.

The mass population is walking around broken hearted, disillusioned, and disconnected as a result of the patriarchy we have been living under. This disconnection from source, from each other and from the earth has caused fear, hatred, distrust, and unimaginable cruelty in our world. We can no longer trust our governments, the police, the media, our bosses, our church leaders, our coaches, our families, our friends, or our spouses. It is a world where fear and distrust have taken such a strong hold on us that most of us do not even realize that we are living in it. We are so busy numbing ourselves that we do not even know that we are breaking.

Is there anyone in your life that you trust implicitly? Someone who you trust with every secret, every dream, every deep shame, every embarrassment, every win, and every fail? Who do trust completely with your body, your heart, and your soul? Who do you completely trust to tell you the truth — good or bad? Is there anyone who you believe in so deeply that you would share your soul wounds and your core values? Do you believe the news? Teachers? Doctors? Who do trust 100% of the time? Do you have someone that you trust to guide you? Someone that believes in you? To be proud of you and not jealous or envy you? Do you believe in humanity? Is the world a good place or evil?

The masculine has built towns, cities,

cars, computers, highways, and houses. The masculine has protected our countries, our rights and our freedoms. They have created what could be and can be an absolute utopia – if we utilize the feminine. 100 years ago, people did not have running water, toilets that flush, washers, and dryers. Most did not have cars, planes did not exist, computers did not exist. We live in such a magical, brilliant, mystical, and creative world and we do not appreciate it! The masculine has done their job – they have been the builders, the architects, they have been the leaders, the defenders, the decision makers, the providers. The masculine has been courageous and strong in their quest for better lives. We should be on our knees grateful every day that we wake up in a bed, in a home, warm, dry, that we can hop into a warm shower and make a pot of coffee and not even think about the absolute fucking magnificence of it all. We are so entitled now that we barely take notice or give gratitude when we do receive what we want, we are happy for a moment and then move onto the next best thing.

The masculine has bled, hurt, sacrificed, and died for what they believe in. They need the feminine to rise, to take their rightful place beside them, no longer behind them, no longer trying to be them. It is long past time that the feminine quit playing a supporting role on this earth and step up to own their power because when the masculine and feminine weave together in each of us, in our society, in our world we will be unfucking stoppable. We will no longer stand for war, terrorism, abuse of power, we will no longer sit by and watch our masculine crumble and fall.

The latest statistics in Canada show that over one million men suffer from major depression each year and that out of the approximate four thousand deaths by suicide, 75% of those are men. Mental health issues are thought of as a weakness, "real men" don't cry, don't ask for help, do not talk about their feelings. This is what this patriarchal society has done to our men and our women. Women who believe that they have to act like men to get ahead are in the exact same situation. Shutting down our feelings is shutting down our roadmap, our guidance system, our feelings are there for a reason and ignoring them is a dangerous game. Our feelings, when ignored get stronger and will show in your body as "dis – ease", stress is the biggest cause of heart problems, obesity, diabetes, headaches, depression, anxiety, gastrointestinal problems and Alzheimer's, and auto immune disease is your body actually fighting itself. When we hold onto and stuff down our anger, our shame, and our resentment it eventually starts to spill over onto others, we project our rage, envy, jealousy, hatred, and fury onto others. We take it out on our spouses, employees, children and even strangers, sometimes not even knowing what triggered such a destructive reaction!

We have been taught to judge our feelings as good and bad – they are neither, they just are. At one end of the scale, you have guilt, shame, hatred, fear – all thought of as bad – and at the other end you have joy, love, happiness – all thought of as good. When we hold ourselves in judgement of the feelings that move through us naturally, we block and stop our growth. How can we grow and change and love ourselves and each other if we believe that our feelings are bad, if we are shamed for how we feel? It is natural to feel the entire scope of feelings, to feel them and let them be our guides not our reactions. We cannot live in shame, guilt, anger, blame, or grief forever, we have to learn how to feel our feelings, acknowledge them and then choose to feel better. When we can see our feelings for what they are, and allow all of them their time, we can heal.

In a world where the masculine and feminine unite, in a world where the patriarch no longer rules, manipulates, bullies and gaslights society, we can and will have an earth we are proud of, an earth that we happily leave to our children. Masculine and feminine united and equal is how we create freedom. Peace, love, compassion, nurturing, and empathy combined with leadership, personal power, strength, and courage is how we create a new world.

Challenges

1) Do you pay attention to your feelings?
2) Do you judge your feelings or feel ashamed of them?
3) Can you believe that you are whole and perfect just the way you are?

You are not broken. You are amazing. We are resilient and strong, and we can and will unite and show the world a better way. The power is within each and every one of us.

CHAPTER ELEVEN

PATRIARCHY

CHAPTER ELEVEN — PATRIARCHY

Our power has been taken away cruelly and endlessly by the Patriarchy. Even in this so-called modern society we live in, the only way women are taken seriously or paid properly is when they act like men, dress like men, essentially becoming masculine with a vagina. Our wild, our adventurous, our sensuous feminine selves have been so completely diminished that most women do not want anything to do with that side of themselves, do not believe that side of them exists or are too afraid to embrace it.

Women have been bartered and sold by their parents, drowned, and murdered for being "just a girl", we have been traded for goats, pigs, cows, donkeys and had absolutely no say. It was not long ago that it was legal for a man to rape, beat, or murder his wife because she was his property. HIS PROPERTY! What the actual fuck?

A woman could not leave or divorce her husband, if a woman had sex before marriage or outside of her marriage, she was branded a whore and cast out, even if her sexual encounter was rape. We were burned at the stake, stoned to death, hung, and betrayed by our sisters, our husbands, our friends! It is no wonder we cower and cringe at the thought of being feminine!! How cruel to be so full of passion, creativity, sensuality, and intuition and have to hide it! To feel ashamed of it! To fear death and betrayal for healing, for loving and for your beauty!

I would love to sit here and say that this has all changed, that this only happened hundreds of years ago but human trafficking, rape, and abuse are at an all-time high! How can we say we live in a civilized society when our children are being beaten, drugged, raped, and bought and sold? The toxic masculine believes that this is his right, that he is powerful because he thinks he is in control. How are we letting this happen? Do you know parts of the human soul that are destroyed by rape? By abuse? By molestation? Do you see where our world needs compassion, love, and freedom? Can you see that embracing our feminine is the way out of this nightmare? Out of this control structure? And into peace. Can you imagine a peaceful world?

One without control and manipulation? I can. I can see a world where my daughter can wear shorts and a tank top to school and not have it be sexualized. I can see a world where my daughter can go to a night club and not worry that she will be drugged and raped if she sets down her drink. I need to believe that together we can raise our sons to quit drugging and raping our daughters, to teach our sons that women are not objects, that they are not pieces of meat, that they are not beneath them. I need to believe that in this society of instant gratification that we are teaching our boys about respect, about empathy, and self-control. I need to believe that we can teach our sons and show our sons that this is unfucking acceptable and teach them, tell them the damage it does. Have the conversations. Teach them what real power is, what a real man is and how to treat girls — no matter how they dress, look, or act.

This patriarchy — this society where the masculine hold all of the power and the feminine are excluded? It has to end; it has to end for our daughters and our sons. This false sense of control they have, with their manipulation of facts, words, religion, education, healthcare, and worst of all the financial sector. Why are there so many unhappy marriages? So many abused women? So many affairs? Because in so many of these cases the feminine has stayed at home, or worked part time, or worked shift work so that they could still take care of their children, their home, and their spouses. These jobs do not usually pay well enough to for a feminine to be able to raise children on their own, so women are stuck in abusive homes trying to raise their children.

The masculine has been taught to believe that if they control the money, they control everything. Money has become something that we have been giving our power away to, it has become a symbol of evil and power and control. Money is none of those things, money is just energy, it is just what we have chosen to use to trade with. The money itself is not good or bad, it is not evil, nor powerful, it is just money. The patriarch and toxic masculine control most of the money world, and their actions, their choices of what to do with that money are evil and controlling, the money doesn't care.

Challenges

1) What areas of your life are you playing the victim, bully, or saviour? Can you step out of the drama circle you are in?
2) What limiting beliefs do you have about money? Do you believe it is the root of all "evil"?
3) What changes can you make in your own family? Your own tribe?

We have lived in this Patriarchal society for so long that most of us believe that this is just what life is. That we are stuck in a Groundhog Day that just keeps repeating itself over and over, but it doesn't have to be like that! We get to choose! We get to change and as we change the world changes.

CHAPTER TWELVE

SACRED WOMB

CHAPTER TWELVE — SACRED WOMB

A woman's womb is sacred. It is where all life begins. Our wombs are our superpower, they are our creativity, our passion, our fertility, and our rebirth. Ix Chel is the Mayan Goddess of the moon, water, healing, childbirth, fertility, creativity, and rebirth, she is the Great Mother – the maiden, mother, and crone. She blesses us with the gifts of fertility, childbirth, healing, and creativity. Our womb is ruled by our sacral chakra – just below your belly button, the color is fire orange, and element is water. The sacral chakra is the energy spiral that regulates our feelings, our sensuality, sexuality, creativity, and our healing powers.

Every sexual encounter you have affects your womb space, whether the encounter is loving or not. When a man enters our sacred womb, we take on more than just their penis, we take on their trauma, their emotions, their DNA, and the trauma, the DNA, and the emotions of their past lovers. Um, why are we not taught this in school?

Did you know this? I did not until recently! This can leave women feeling ashamed, closed off and uncertain how to heal or how to accept our own personal sexual feelings. This is the just the trauma we have consensually allowed in, so what happens when a woman is forced to have sex? Whether they are manipulated, drugged, sold, or raped... what happens to the womb then? Where does that guilt, shame, fear, hatred, depression, and anxiety go? If untreated it does not go anywhere. It stays stuck in womb, in your sacral chakra and when your sacral chakra is not balanced your emotions go crazy, you become either over or under sexual, your creativity is blocked, your sexuality and your "gut" instincts are blocked. If your emotions are completely out of control, you may need to heal your womb. *(I have a 4-week cleansing, clearing & womb activation available — check www.doubleinfinityhealing.ca)*

We are given a million mixed messages on being sexy, sexual, and sensual. We have been taught to be ashamed of our desires, to hide our wants and needs, to be good girls, and to let men be in charge. We are shamed for our sexual encounters as either sluts or frigid, there is no middle ground. If we are too demanding, too powerful, too sexual, too forward in the bedroom our partners feel like we are taking away their masculinity, but if we are too timid and just lie there, then we are boring and have no passion. I am happy to say that more and more conversations about sex – from both men and women – are starting to show up, making us feel less alone in our wants and needs in the bedroom. We are all built different and like sex in different ways, speeds, styles – we are not a one size, or position, or speed fits all.

Are you withholding pleasure from yourself as a punishment for something in your past? A past lover? A past desire? A past assault? Are you holding shame in your womb because you were never taught that it is safe to ask for what you want? That it isn't safe to have desires? Are you faking orgasms? Do you masturbate? Do you feel safe to be naked, completely naked in front of your lover? In front of your mirror? Where did you learn that your pleasure was wrong or not important?

We have learned to put conditions on love, on how it is given, received, who deserves it and who doesn't, on how we express it and how it is expressed back. We put limitations on love coming in, love going out and on how much we can love ourselves. When we put conditions on love, we block all of the rest of our gifts, when we judge others as not lovable, we are closing our hearts, when we have been hurt beyond our wildest imagination and we stop loving and trusting ourselves and others we are giving our power away. Have you ever been shamed about your body, sex, sexuality, your looks, your past sexual encounters? Do you regret or wish to forget any of your past experiences?

Are you ready to show up as the healed, divinely sexual, and sensual, intuitive, creative person that you are truly meant to be? Would you believe me if I told that healing your womb is one of the fastest ways to manifest? That your sexual energy is the most powerful manifesting energy that there is? So, what does that mean for your manifesting if you are blocked? It means your abundance is blocked – this can be wealth, health, relationships, whatever your deepest desires are!

Law of attraction is way more in depth

than repeating mantras over and over. It is more than "act like you have it and it will show up," or "think abundance all day long." One of the key elements of manifestation that seems to get left out are the feelings, the emotions. If you cannot feel the love, the excitement, the wonder, or the passion of what you are desiring you can't manifest it! If you are just chanting mantras and not feeling them, believing them, or loving them, nothing will change. Toxic positivity is pretending to be in flow, love, happiness, and joy all of the time! "I am love! I am light! I am sunshine! I am happiness!" Ugh. Nobody, well 95% of us anyway, are not that level of happiness all of the time. We all have highs and lows and when we pretend that we don't we are lying to ourselves and setting unrealistic expectations for those around us.

Clearing our sacral chakra and our womb space allows us to feel, to really feel our emotions. It opens us up to our sexual, sensual, creative and our emotional selves. We feel our "gut" instincts again and learn how to follow that feeling of knowing. When we learn to understand our feelings and emotions and "know" what we want, we step into our power. Our personal power, our manifesting power, our emotional mastery and into self-love. When our creative energy and our other feminine energies flow at their full potential our ability to change our lives is unstoppable.

Do you believe that you are totally responsible for your life? That your thoughts and feelings create your reality? Do you understand that like attracts like? How does it feel to look in a mirror and own all of your choices and decisions and know that you created this life? Are you ready to choose different?

Challenges

1) Heal your womb space!
2) Love your body, feel deeply and completely grateful for everything it does for you!
3) How do you feel about sex? Pleasure? Sensuality?

Sex has been used to victimize, to manipulate, and to control women. Are you ready to stand in your feminine? Are you ready to step into your own personal sensuality and sexuality?

CHAPTER THIRTEEN

LIMITLESS
POSSIBILITIES

CHAPTER THIRTEEN — LIMITLESS POSSIBILITIES

Everything is energy. Everything. We are energy and we have several different energy systems within us. We have chakras – seven main ones that start at your tailbone and go up to your crown. We also have meridians; they are the energetic highway of the body. Meridians allow for the flow of energy to move and circulate throughout the body (also known as Qi). We also have radiant circuits (see *Donna Eden*) they are a series of energetic flows in the body, they are our joy pathways although they are different than Meridians in that they don't have set paths. When your radiant circuits are flowing properly, they send joy throughout your entire body.

Masculine and Feminine are also energies in our bodies and we can embody and balance them within ourselves. Society has taught us that we are either a man or a woman, that we like blue or we like pink, that we are strong, or we are weak, that we like trucks or we like Barbies™.

If a male likes anything considered girly he is bullied and called a sissy, girly boy, pansy – God the list goes on and on – big boys don't cry, cowboy up, suck it up butter cup! And girls, if they like trucks, or short hair, or wearing jeans, they are tomboys, cross dressers, butchy and on and on. Girls have also been told they are oversensitive, too emotional, and that they feel too much. Remember feelings are our roadmaps, our compasses, so how the hell are we supposed to follow our roadmap when we are constantly being shamed for having one? When we are mocked and ridiculed for any and all emotions that make others feel uncomfortable? We are so programmed to care more about what others think than how we feel, we don't want to embarrass ourselves by crying in front of people, or shouting, we do not under any circumstances want to make other people uncomfortable. It is insanity. It is also one of the biggest reasons that we are in a complete mental health crisis. We are too afraid of looking weak, losing control, and of judgement to ask for help, to cry in front of others, to lose our cool or to show compassion and empathy.

When we are not in balance, and we try to work together we end up bumping and pushing and tugging and trying to control each other. Imagine dancing with someone – the first dance is two people, both fully in their masculine, they are both trying to lead, both trying to control the movement and the directions, both wanting to make the choices and both wanting to win. They would end up in a fist fight because neither would lessen their grip or give up one ounce of their control or power. War – two masculine personalities not wanting to lose. In marriage if there are two masculine personalities it is a constant power struggle, they both know what they want and they want it their way. Now imagine two feminine dancing – there would be no direction, no steps, no leader, no flow. We would never make decisions or know what direction to go if we were all fully in our feminine. In a marriage with two feminine it is stagnant, no one wants to make a decision or change anything, there is no adventure.

If we can balance our masculine and feminine energies within ourselves and our relationships, we can change our lives. It is the way all life is meant to be. Give and take, Yin and Yang, dark and light, breathe in and breathe out, day and night, hot and cold. We are not meant to live in one or the other at all times. We are meant to be in balance, to live in balance and to love in balance. Sometimes we have to lead with our masculine and sometimes we have to lead with our feminine, different situations provide us with different responses. Children usually go to their moms when they are sick because women are naturally more nurturing, healing, and compassionate – but men can and do also show up for their children in this way – it just is not their natural energy. Children usually go to their dads if they need to build something or have a career question because men are usually more decisive and more hands on – again women can also build things and make decisions. These are just examples of our natural tendencies; they do not mean that we cannot or should not move in between the two energies.

Sometimes we lead and sometimes we follow. If we are always leading and controlling then we can miss some of the sweeter things, the little magical things and if we are always following, we can forget what we like, what we desire and even who we are. There are some things I hate make decisions on. Eating out for example. My husband loves food, good food, he loves trying new things and new places. I could care less about food, I am just as happy with a Big Mac as a $200.00 meal, so I usually let him choose. I also let him choose our hikes, as long as it is on a mountain and it won't kill me, I'm happy to just embrace it. But Decorating? Kids? TV shows? We plan together. For vacations, budgets and pets, I take the lead... (I would have geese, goats and llamas if I did not.)

We are not perfect but the decision to write this book came about because we do share the workload. I was actually shocked to see how many women still think they have to or want to do it all. My husband cooks, cleans, helps with the kids, does yard work, and fixes things around the house. He decorates for Christmas, organizes our adventures, and works hard so that our kids and I can follow our dreams. I also work hard, cook, clean, do yard work, manage our finances, and create a comfortable home. We have a system, there are things he does that I do not, and things I do that he does not, but in the middle we work together. If he is having a bad week, I do a little extra, if I am glued to my computer writing this book, he does a little extra. We appreciate what each of us brings to the relationship. We are flexible in our give and take and in our receiving.

Are you open to receive in your relationships? If you are always giving you will end up either burnt out or resentful or both. You have to be open to receive help, love, money, emotional support and even advice. Receiving is very feminine and absolutely one of the biggest aspects that has been lost to most humans. We stop the flow of love, money, health, joy, and all aspects of abundance because we do not know how to receive, how to be open. Our pride, our egos tell us to do it ourselves, do not take charity, give don't take. Most of us can barely receive a compliment gracefully or allow a friend to buy us lunch. Being able to give and receive is a perfect example of masculine and feminine energies working in sync.

Challenges

1) How do you want to experience yourself?
2) Try being in the receiving mode for a week, see how it feels to be open and available to receive.
3) Can you practice giving and receiving with gratitude this week? Watch how relationships flow differently.

Do you believe that we are limitless? That life is full of possibilities? Do you believe that life is meant to be lived, not to be tolerated? Embrace your life! Say yes to all of the possibilities, all of the dreams, and all that you are! Freedom lives in our limitlessness, it lives in the alignment of our masculine and feminine, it lives in us. What does freedom mean to you?

CHAPTER FOURTEEN

ABUSE

Fuck anyone who ever made you believe that you are hard to love. You do not need to prove your worthiness to anyone, ever. Do not let anyone break your heart and your trust so completely that you lose yourself, lose the ability to trust yourself or lose yourself in the grief. Did you know that agreeing to do things that you do not want to do to keep the peace is a trauma response? You can use your voice and take back your power! No longer allow them to strip away your worthiness, layer by layer – until you no longer exist, until you don't recognize who is looking back at you in the mirror.

Anyone can be an abusee or an abuser. If you are trying to control another person by withholding something it is abuse. If you withhold love, money, sex, affection, kindness, or any type of intimacy from anyone if they don't do what you want, it is abuse. The only thing that is ever really in our control is ourselves, our feelings, and our reactions to things! When we try to control others or manipulate them it becomes a very damaging type of abuse. Usually, people try to control or manipulate others because they feel powerless somewhere in their lives and have low self-esteem. People with anxiety often use control as a way to cope and maintain balance in their lives without even realizing the affect that it has on others. Trauma left untreated can show up as control – they had no control in a situation so now they compensate by trying to control everything in their environment including the people. Abuse is a masculine trait, the need for control, the need to win, the need to lead.

The healed feminine will never surrender to the wounded masculine. If the feminine is being bullied, controlled, abused, cheated on, belittled, dishonoured, manipulated, or attacked, her masculine, her inner masculine will rise. Her masculine will not allow this treatment and will rise to guard the feminine.

The healed masculine will never surrender to the wounded feminine. If the masculine is being seduced, lied to, cheated on, disconnected, or is having sex withheld, he will walk away. He will not look back.

If you are in a relationship where there is abuse, ask yourself why you allow it. Why do you allow yourself to be abused, controlled, gaslighted, bullied, manipulated, cheated on, lied to and codependent? Why do you allow yourself to be a victim in this role? Are there other places in your life that you allow yourself to be a victim? Are you afraid to use your masculine energies to set boundaries? Do you think that the feminine is meant to be weak or malleable? What would it take for you to trust yourself and your own decisions? Can you love yourself enough to try?

Begging someone to love you is the most painful thing you will ever do. Whether it is begging to be treated kindly, compassionately, and lovingly or begging them to respect you, it is begging for love.

Begging someone to stay with you is soul crushing. Begging someone to believe in you is heartbreaking. If they want to leave you, let them go, if they want to control you, let them go, if they want to be with someone else, let them. Do not beg for love. Do not sacrifice your self-worth to keep someone who is does not want to be with you. The feminine believes so strongly in forgiveness and compassion that they often stay too long in unhealthy relationships and they forget to show it to themselves.

Gaslighting is a way that people control others. It can be parents, bosses, friends, or spouses, and it is so dangerous because it is such a skilled method of manipulation. Gaslighting can be super sneaky and unnoticeable at first... but it is an absolute evil powerplay. The person gaslighting will subtly make the other person, or people believe that they are losing their minds, their sanity, and their sense of reality. They will convince the others that things were not said or done the way they think they were. They will even joke about them "losing their minds". They will play the victim and make others feel like they are the bully. They will make the others believe that their feelings are either too big or too small depending on the situation – but never ever appropriate. They lie and manipulate easily; they make others feel stupid and foolish. Gaslighting is the fastest way to gain control over others, it diminishes their self-respect, self-worth, identity, and it makes others question the core of who they are. They will turn others against you, make sure that they are supported in case someone sees through them. It is a dangerous manipulation and leaves people questioning what is real and what is not.

Physical and sexual abuse are traits of toxic masculinity, believing that they are in control and hold all of the power. They believe that they have the right to abuse others because they believe that they are above them, own them, or are more important than them. This false sense of ownership makes them believe that they have the right to discipline others however they see fit. The toxic masculine is really only insecure when they know that the other person deserves better.

Never love someone so much that fixing them destroys you. Choose you first, then others – you cannot fill someone up if you are empty inside. You get to choose to feel better in every moment. When you are stressed out, or anxious about your future, you are stressed out about something you are only imaging. If you are worried about your future take a look at worse case scenarios. What is the absolute worst case scenario you can imagine... would you survive it? If you are depressed or living in grief, shame, or blame, you are living in a past that no longer exists except in your mind. You cannot change the past and living there can be painstaking. Release yourself from the past, from any would-haves, could-haves or should-haves. Look at the memory you are holding on to, did anything good at all come out of the situation? Can you find a lesson? A silver lining?

No amount of security is worth the suffering of abuse, gaslighting, manipulation, or control. No amount of security is worth living in these conditions of fear, guilt, and shame, chained to a life that has killed your passion and your dreams. When you are degraded, blamed, humiliated, and seeking someone else's approval you quit believing in you. You quit believing that you are strong, bold, powerful, and filled with the magic of infinite possibility and potential. Can you trust yourself? Your choices? Your instincts? When did you quit? The feminine is intuitive and we fear this – we have been taught to fear it, to be ashamed, and to hide it. It is not woo woo, or witch craft, it is actually one of our senses — our 6th sense. We are created to trust our guts, our instincts and ourselves. So, let's start believing in ourselves and loving ourselves, lets honour ourselves and set better examples for our children.

Challenges

1) If you are in an abusive relationship – please seek help! Now.
2) If you have quit believing in the magic of you – start remembering! Remember who you are! You are perfectly you! You are a miracle; you are here on this earth for a reason!
3) What are your top 5 passions? What are your top 5 gifts? What are your top 5 skills? What are your top 5 values? These are your purpose, this is your path!

It is time for all of us to look in a mirror. To look at our beliefs and our behaviours to see if they still serve us. Does it serve you to control others? Or to be controlled by others? Are you living a life that you are proud of? Are you the type of man or woman that you would like your son or daughter to date? Self-love is honouring the truth of who you are and making decisions from what is real to you in this moment. This transformation into self-love breaks old patterns of self-sabotage and creates new possibilities.

CHAPTER FIFTEEN

SELF-LOVE

CHAPTER FIFTEEN — SELF-LOVE

Let go of who you think you should be. Quit breaking your own heart by trying to be someone you are not, by trying to hold on to something or someone who is ready to leave. Imagine being loved the way that you love others and love yourself like that. You are perfectly you. You are perfectly you exactly who you are right now! Rise above the fear and embrace your feminine and your masculine! Own them both! You are both and you are the master of your energy, your emotions, and your life. You have everything you want inside of you; you do not need a partner or anyone else to complete you, you are both masculine and feminine and can call upon them both at any time. You are whole and complete; you were born a perfect miracle and you still are one. You do not have to be perfect for anyone but you – you are perfectly you – you cannot be anyone else and no one else can be you.

What stories did you grow up with about who you should be? These are stories we get from our parents, teachers, coaches, friends, church leaders and other family members. There are also stories about how we should look. Magazines and movies show us a different perfect look every couple of years – for men and for women. Outdoorsy and sporty or classic or bohemian or trendy. We cannot possibly keep up or change to what the trendy look of the year is, but we spend thousands of dollars trying!

Were you told you are too short? Too tall? Too flat or too curvy? Were you told you were stupid because you are blonde or could not do math or science because you are a girl? Were you teased for being a sensitive boy or girl? For crying or feeling empathy? Were you told that you were dumb or ugly or flat or not worth loving? Did someone take away your power? Did you feel unlovable? Unworthy? Or unimportant when you were growing up? Do you still believe those old stories? Those opinions from one unempowered human? The opinion from someone who may not even remember who you are? Who is still holding that power over you? That power that when you look in the mirror you know they were right? Big nose, buck teeth, small eyes, big forehead, big ears, bald, hairy, fat, flat, ugly, girly, goofy. Do you still hear their voice telling you this? Can you still feel the pain and humiliation? Is it time to let it go? All of that baggage, hurt, shame and embarrassment? Are you ready to take back your power?

Self-love is a choice and commitment. It is about being devoted to you. It is not a glass of wine and a bubble bath once a month, it is you choosing you in every single experience. It is about setting boundaries and being authentically you. Self-love is about being in integrity to yourself. Do you promise yourself to lose weight, quit drinking, smoking, get in shape, meditate, or do yoga and never do it? Or do for a couple of days and then quit? How can you be trustworthy if you cannot even keep your word to yourself? How do you sabotage yourself? Do you procrastinate, get too busy, forget, or just ignore? How is this serving you? This is where masculine and feminine energies work amazing together! Use these energies to love yourself more – Make a plan (M) Create (F) Visualize (F) Set a schedule (M) Love yourself (F) Do the work (M) Celebrate (F) Self-love means taking care of yourself mentally, emotionally, and physically. You matter, you are worthy, and you are worth the time and effort.

Love where you are right here, right now. Love the essence of you and the core of you. We have been taught to hate our bodies, to judge our bodies and other bodies. We have been taught to be ashamed of how our bodies look, feel, and react. Be fearless in being completely you, your look, your style, your dreams, and your passions! Be so sure of yourself in your own life that you do not need to shame or blame or envy anyone else. Love your wild, audacious, magical, silly self so much that others feel free to love theirs too! Choose to be authentically you!

Learning to love ourselves is a beautiful, inspiring journey. It shows us our magic and our passions and our hearts. The very best thing about loving ourselves is it teaches others how we deserve to be treated. So how do we learn to love ourselves when we have been taught that it is vain, or egotistical, or selfish to put ourselves first? Start where you are and love up! Find a coach, a mentor, a numerologist, or some type of guide to help you if you do not know how to start. *(I have listed some names at the back of the book for some suggestions if you need them – I also have a Midlife Awakening course available.)*

I coach people to start small, add little bits in at time – taking care of mind, body, and spirit! I teach forgiveness and gratitude as the first steppingstones.

For the body – start with adding something in that is good for you, even if it starts with just an extra glass of water. Move your body! There are a million options here! You do not have to go to a gym, or run, or do yoga! Find something that you love enough to stick to it! Dance, hike, swim, Qi gong, rock climb, group sports, walking, hula hooping, chakra dance!! Oh, I could go on and on, but you get the idea!

For the mind – keep it active! Learn something new! There are courses all over the internet! You can learn virtually anything online! Read a book or go back to school! Keep your mind sharp!

For the spirit – I could work on my spirit all day long! Here are my favourites – Breathwork, Emotional

Freedom Technique, Meditation, Qi gong, Reiki, *Donna Eden* – energy medicine! Just to name a few!

Learn to love yourself when you are naked. Dance naked in front of the mirror. Look at yourself naked and see how wonderful the human body is! Appreciate everything it has done for you! Love it for keeping you alive with very little maintenance. Love yourself and your body enough to make better choices, to be healthier, to be calmer, to be happy.

Be bold, be unique, be perfectly you!

Challenges

1) Move your body! Make it fun! Love how your body looks, feels, and moves!
2) Learn something new – anything! You can learn anything from cooking, to playing guitar, to quantum healing online!
3) Take time for your spirit! Meditate, Breathwork, Yoga! Find your peaceful practice!

As we learn to love ourselves our world changes, we are no longer willing to accept mediocre! We look for new possibilities and new paths to forge every day! We quit believing in limits and start living in limitlessness!

THE MASCULINE AND FEMININE: TOGETHER AT LAST

CHAPTER SIXTEEN — THE MASCULINE AND FEMININE: TOGETHER AT LAST

Your choices are not a life sentence. You can choose at any time to change. You can step out of your life and into a new one at any time, the decisions you made when you were 20 do not have to be the road map for your entire life. You can change jobs, where you live, friendships, spouses, your look, your style, your money story and even your masculine and feminine energies. You are not stuck with your old choices and old ways of thinking or being.

Embracing your masculine and feminine is a choice. We are equal! We are not here to be in some twisted competition, we are not better than or worse than, we are not stronger than or weaker than. We are different, we are all so completely different and that is what makes the earth so absolutely fucking amazing! It is what gives us our strengths and how we learn!

We are all so afraid to walk the path of the feminine, the path of love, nurturing, healing, compassion, and empathy! The path of our ancestors where we dance and sing and celebrate ourselves and each other. We are so terrified to be shamed or judged for being sexual, sensual, unique, or different, that we have all tried to fit ourselves into these tiny, itty-bitty lives that suffocate us! These are not our weaknesses; these are our strengths! We take these strengths and stuff them down and try to be more masculine, more assertive, more go getters, more in charge. We burn our bras and change words so that we feel more equal – it has become a rivalry between sexes rather than a partnership. We cannot all look like the newest cover of a magazine, we cannot all be sporty, outdoorsy, classy, sexy, feminine, masculine, tall, short, curvy, flat, blonde, brunette, redheads, with blue, green, and brown eyes all at the same time.

Quit judging yourself. You really do get to be perfectly you even if you have things you would like to change. Quit judging others. If you get to be perfectly you then let others be perfectly them. It is not your job to change another person and trying to change someone else (unless they ask for help) is a form of control. You cannot control anything outside of yourself. You cannot change anyone other than yourself. You cannot change what is happening around you, you can only change how you react to it. Control your emotions, your reactions, your fight, flight, or freeze responses and your knee jerk reflexes and you change the script. You are in charge; you get to choose how you engage and when you disengage.

If we all took control of our own lives and our own happiness and quit expecting to be rescued or saved or loved or appreciated by someone outside of ourselves, we would see how magnificent we are. If we quit judging ourselves and others and quit fearing judgement or condemnation from others how free would we feel? How free would we feel if we could just love ourselves exactly how we are? If we could love and embrace our masculine and feminine energies completely? How much more love could we feel if we filled our hearts first and then shared that love with others?

Do you believe that peace, love, happiness, and abundance are only real in movies and fairy tales? Do you believe in magic of love, gratitude, forgiveness, and absolute acceptance for every single being on the planet? Do you believe that we can change the earth by loving ourselves, loving each other, and loving all things?

My Vagina doesn't do the dishes, it doesn't scrub the toilets or wash the floors. My Vagina does not make me weaker, softer, stupider, less than or a slave. My Vagina does not make me an object for men to disrespect or a piece of meat to be bartered or sold. When my Vagina says NO it means NO – I don't fucking care who you are! My Vagina does not make me have to obey or shut up any longer. Your vagina does not do the dishes either!

Are you ready to be the change that we have been waiting for? Are you willing to embrace your feminine and bring much needed love, compassion, and healing to the earth? Do believe that the feminine is the "peace" that has been missing? I do. The feminine are learning to play by their own rules, making their own way in this masculine dominant world.

Love yourself, love your family, love your life, and love our world! Quit looking at things that the Patriarch are showing us to keep us in fear, the news, the magazines, and social media. Look at your life. Look in your neighbourhoods, in your groups, in your family and see the good, the compassion, and the love. Look at what is real. Feel the heartbeat of the earth and show her your love and respect. The world is amazing, beautiful, and limitless in its possibilities! Imagine, believe, and embrace your future – your future with a perfect understanding, a perfect balance, and a perfect union of your masculine and feminine.

Let your masculine and feminine join together and let the adventures begin.

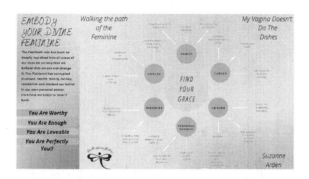

— The End —

REFERENCES

Suzanne Arden

www.doubleinfinityhealing.ca

Breathwork coach, Life coach, Sacred Womb Healing, Midlife Awakening 16 week course

Shelly Anderson

www.shellyanderson-sacredawakenings .com

Quantum Numerologist

Elle Odin

www.elleodyn.com

Business Infusion sessions, Quantum Numerology, Mastering the BrainGAME

"RUN FROM WHAT'S
COMFORTABLE,
FORGET SAFETY.
LIVE WHERE YOU FEAR TO LIVE.
DESTROY YOUR REPUTATION.
BE NOTORIOUS."

— RUMI

Printed in the United States
by Baker & Taylor Publisher Services